CONTENTS

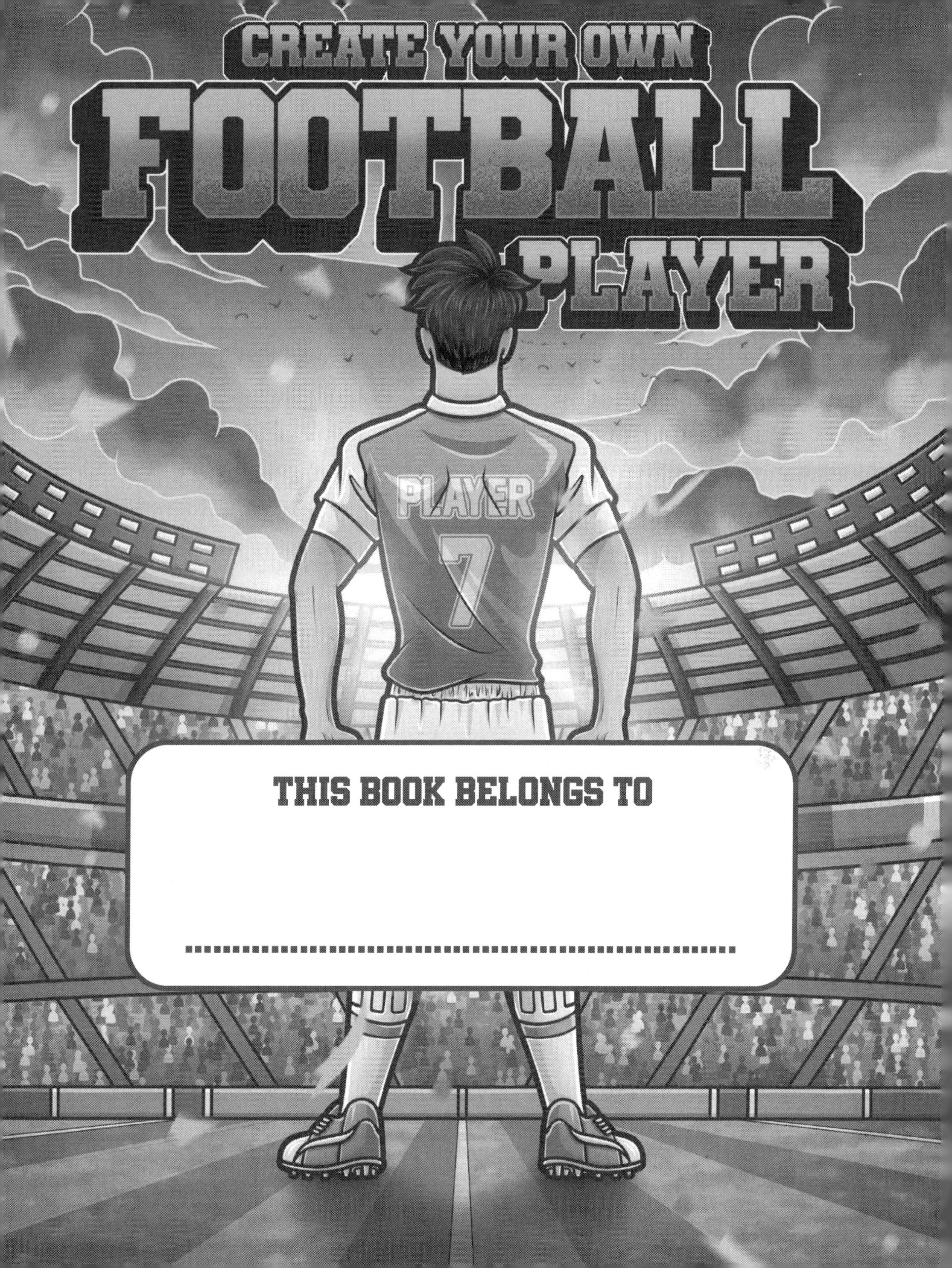
CREATE YOUR OWN
FOOTBALL
PLAYER
PLAYER
7
THIS BOOK BELONGS TO

Thank you for purchasing this book from amberoctopus, we hope you enjoy it.

Based in rural Buckinghamshire, amberoctopus is a small business created by a father of two young daughters. Our aim is to create engaging books for young people that spark their imagination and creativity – as well as giving parents a little break.

Please consider leaving a review on Amazon. This support will help us create more quality books in the future, thank you very much.

Visit **amberoctopus.com** for more information and to view our full range of books.

PLAYER PROFILE

Complete your player profile below

Name: ....

Age: ....

Height: ....

Weight: ....

City of birth: ....

Nationality: ....

Position: ....

Left/right footed: ....

Preferred shirt number: ....

Favourite team: ....

Favourite player: ....

Favourite manager: ....

Most disliked team: ....

Most disliked player: ....

Welcome to the start of what promises to be an amazing football career. To begin with, complete your player information.

STATS CARD

Rating

Position

National flag

Name

Shooting

Dribbling

Passing

Tackling

Pace

Strength

You have been invited for a trial at local third division club, Oakshire Town. Before the trial, you'll need to clean your boots! Can you spot the FIVE differences between the two football boots? Once you have spotted all the differences, colour in the boots ready for your trial.

SPOT THE DIFFERENCE

Time for you to impress on the pitch! Starting at the cones, make your way through the maze to collect the football and shoot past the goalkeeper.

START

When signing new players, the club looks for many different skills. Can you find all the skills in the wordsearch?

SKILLS

Z	U	W	V	P	A	S	S	I	N	G	O
E	P	V	G	B	D	J	N	V	C	X	L
C	G	A	I	C	D	S	W	P	R	T	E
O	K	K	C	S	R	H	Y	K	S	E	A
N	W	A	U	E	I	O	C	H	T	A	D
T	N	B	D	H	B	O	V	J	R	M	E
R	T	S	M	W	B	T	N	X	E	W	R
O	T	A	C	K	L	I	N	G	N	O	S
L	S	F	Q	X	I	N	E	D	G	R	H
H	E	A	D	I	N	G	B	S	T	K	I
D	G	U	F	X	G	Q	D	R	H	M	P
Q	C	E	C	R	O	S	S	I	N	G	Z

HEADING
SHOOTING
PASSING
TACKLING
PACE
STRENGTH
LEADERSHIP
DRIBBLING
VISION
CROSSING
TEAMWORK
CONTROL

Congratulations! After impressing in your trial, the club are delighted to offer you a contract. However, FIVE words in the contract have been scrambled. Can you unscramble the underlined words? Once complete, sign and date the contract.

1 ____________________ 2 ____________________

3 ____________________ 4 ____________________

5 ____________________

SKILLS

Z	U	W	V	P	A	S	S	I	N	G	O
E	P	V	G	B	D	J	N	V	C	X	L
C	G	A	I	C	D	S	W	P	R	T	E
O	K	K	C	S	R	H	Y	K	S	E	A
N	W	A	U	E	I	O	C	H	T	A	D
T	N	B	D	H	B	O	V	J	R	M	E
R	T	S	M	W	B	T	N	X	E	W	R
O	T	A	C	K	L	I	N	G	N	O	S
L	S	F	Q	X	I	N	E	D	G	R	H
H	E	A	D	I	N	G	B	S	T	K	I
D	G	U	F	X	G	Q	D	R	H	M	P
Q	C	E	C	R	O	S	S	I	N	G	Z

HEADING
SHOOTING
PASSING
TACKLING
PACE
STRENGTH
LEADERSHIP
DRIBBLING
VISION
CROSSING
TEAMWORK
CONTROL

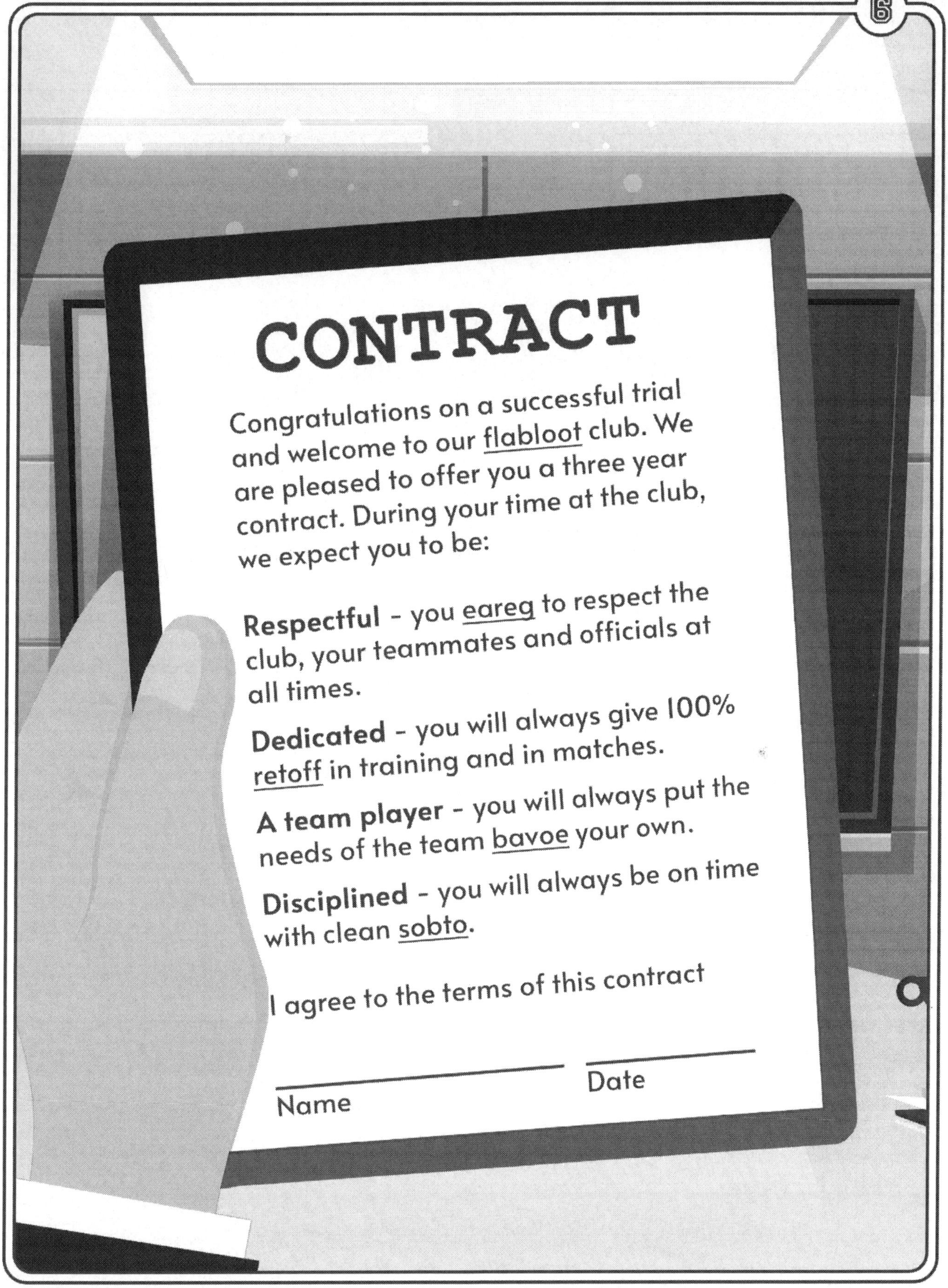

CONTRACT

Congratulations on a successful trial and welcome to our flabloot club. We are pleased to offer you a three year contract. During your time at the club, we expect you to be:

Respectful - you eareg to respect the club, your teammates and officials at all times.

Dedicated - you will always give 100% retoff in training and in matches.

A team player - you will always put the needs of the team bavoe your own.

Disciplined - you will always be on time with clean sobto.

I agree to the terms of this contract

____________________ ________________

Name Date

You have been selected in the matchday squad for tonight's match at Green Park Stadium. Using the grid as a guide, copy the drawing to create your own stadium.

Congratulations! After impressing in your trial, the club are delighted to offer you a contract. However, FIVE words in the contract have been scrambled. Can you unscramble the underlined word? Once complete, sign and date the contract.

1 football

2 agree

3 effort

4 above

5 boots

COPY THE STADIUM

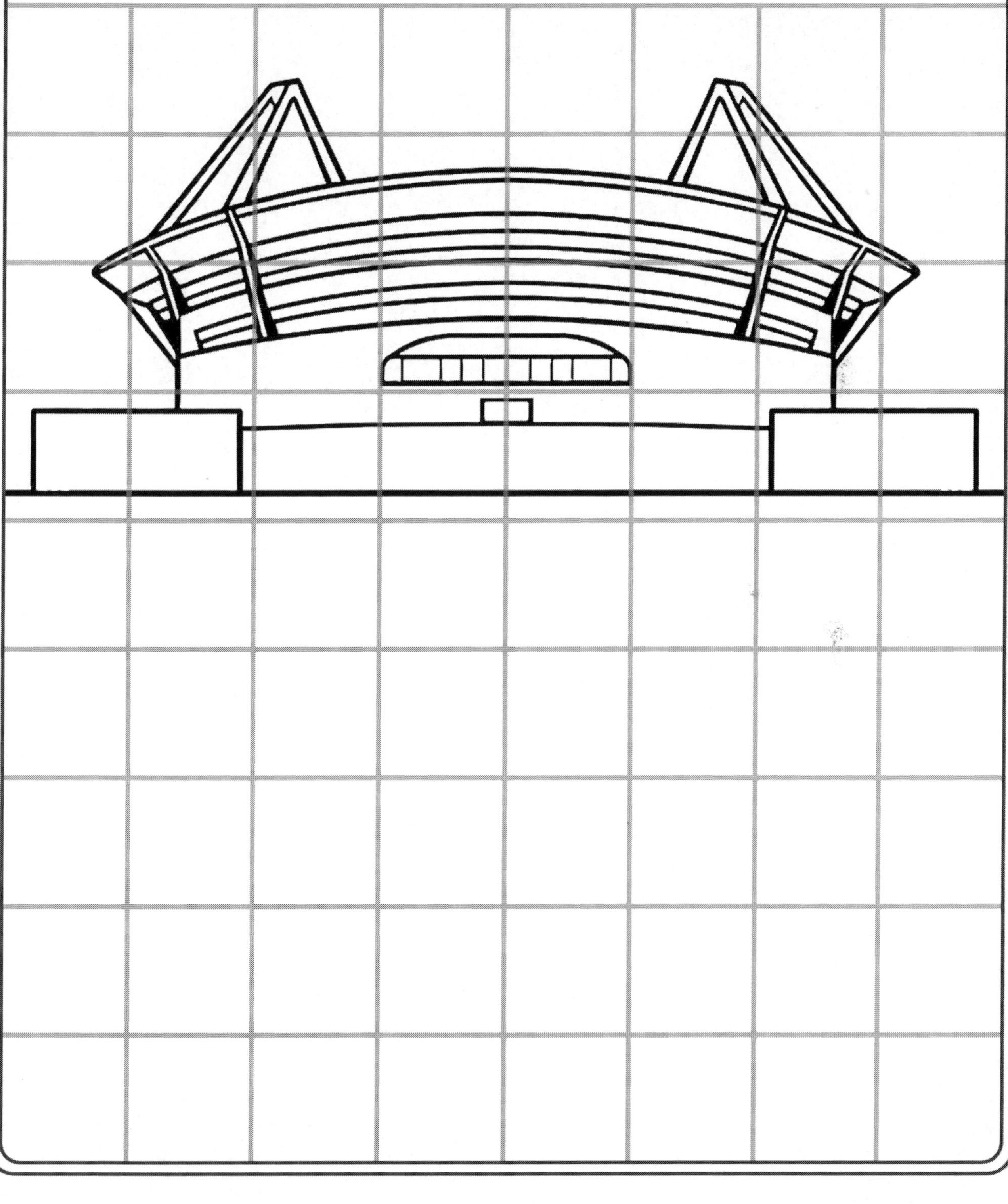

You're all set to make your debut. Design the kit and get ready for the match!

GOOOOOOOAAAAAAAALLLLLLLLL!
A goal on your debut, well played!
Complete the dot to dot goal celebration and colour in the picture.

1
2
3
4
5
6
7
8
9
10
11
12
13
14
15
16
17
18
19
20
21
22
23
24
25
26
27
28
29
30
31
32
33
34
35
36
37
38
39
40
41
42
43
44
45
46
47
48
49
50

Your debut performance has made the front page of the local newspaper. Due to an error, some letters are missing from the article. Can you identify the missing letters to create a word?

__ __ __ __ __ __ __ __

Sunday 12 August - Issue 734 - www.localdailynews.web - £1.80

DAILY NEWS

DEBUT DYNAMO

In an exciting match, our new player celebrated their _irst game with an awesome goal that w_n the match. Everyone in the stadium was really happy, watching this new player sh_w amazing skills and teamwork.

The coolest part happened when the game was almost finished. With some grea_ moves and lots of determination, the new player kicked the _all into the net, and everyone cheered like crazy. We were definitely watching a superstar in the making, _nd we can't wait to see more of their awesome football skills!

So, keep your eyes on the pitch because there are sure to be more thrilling goa_s and fantastic moments from this young ta_ent in the future!

Max's Bus Adventure

Max, the playful pup, found himself far from home after chasing a squirrel. Spotting a bus, he hopped on for a surprise ride. With a wagging tail, Max made friends with passengers as the bus rumbled along.

Meanwhile, Max's worried family searched everywhere. Just as they were about to lose hope, the bus brought Max back to familiar territory. With a joyful bark, Max hopped off, reuniting with his relieved family. Max's unexpected bus ride turned into a heartwarming journey of adventure and reunion!

It's the last game of the season and to win the league, your team must win this match. However, you're 2-0 down at half time. Can you score the three goals your team needs to win the match?

Your debut performance has made the front page of the local newspaper. Due to an error, some letters are missing from the article. Can you identify the missing letters to create a word?

f o o t b a l l

What a performance! Your hat-trick guided the team to the league title. Use the grid to complete the image of you celebrating with your medal.

COMPLETE THE DRAWING

After a brilliant season, you have been signed by second division side, Elmridge FC. Design the badge of your new club.

DESIGN THE BADGE

It's your first training session with your new manager. Spot the SIX differences between the two images. Then colour the manager in.

You're all set for the new season with your new team. Find all the league's teams in the wordsearch.

LEAGUE TABLE

H	H	J	M	P	B	P	E	W	R	A	O
H	A	F	K	S	R	L	L	A	M	I	H
E	R	V	W	S	I	A	M	L	O	P	E
A	R	Z	E	L	C	R	R	D	S	R	D
T	O	P	D	N	K	K	I	E	S	I	G
H	W	C	C	T	F	S	D	N	W	V	E
V	G	W	R	R	I	I	G	W	O	E	B
A	A	Z	K	E	E	D	E	S	O	R	R
L	T	E	V	Q	L	E	T	L	D	D	O
E	E	C	B	G	D	S	O	X	D	A	O
M	E	A	D	O	W	S	I	D	E	L	K
M	A	P	L	E	W	O	O	D	L	E	F

1. BRICKFIELD
2. ELMRIDGE
3. HARROWGATE
4. HAVENFIELD
5. HEATHVALE
6. HEDGEBROOK
7. LARKSIDE
8. MAPLEWOOD
9. MEADOWSIDE
10. MOSSWOOD
11. RIVERDALE
12. WALDEN

Complete the dot to dot and score a goal with a bicycle kick. You can also colour the image in if you like.

15

LEAGUE TABLE

H	H	J	M	P	B	P	E	W	R	A	O
H	A	F	K	S	R	L	L	A	M	I	H
E	R	V	W	S	I	A	M	L	O	P	E
A	R	Z	E	L	C	R	R	D	S	R	D
T	O	P	D	N	K	K	I	E	S	I	G
H	W	C	C	T	F	S	D	N	W	V	E
V	G	W	R	R	I	I	G	W	O	E	B
A	A	Z	K	E	E	D	E	S	O	R	R
L	T	E	V	Q	L	E	T	L	D	D	O
E	E	C	B	G	D	S	O	X	D	A	O
M	E	A	D	O	W	S	I	D	E	L	K
M	A	P	L	E	W	O	O	D	L	E	F

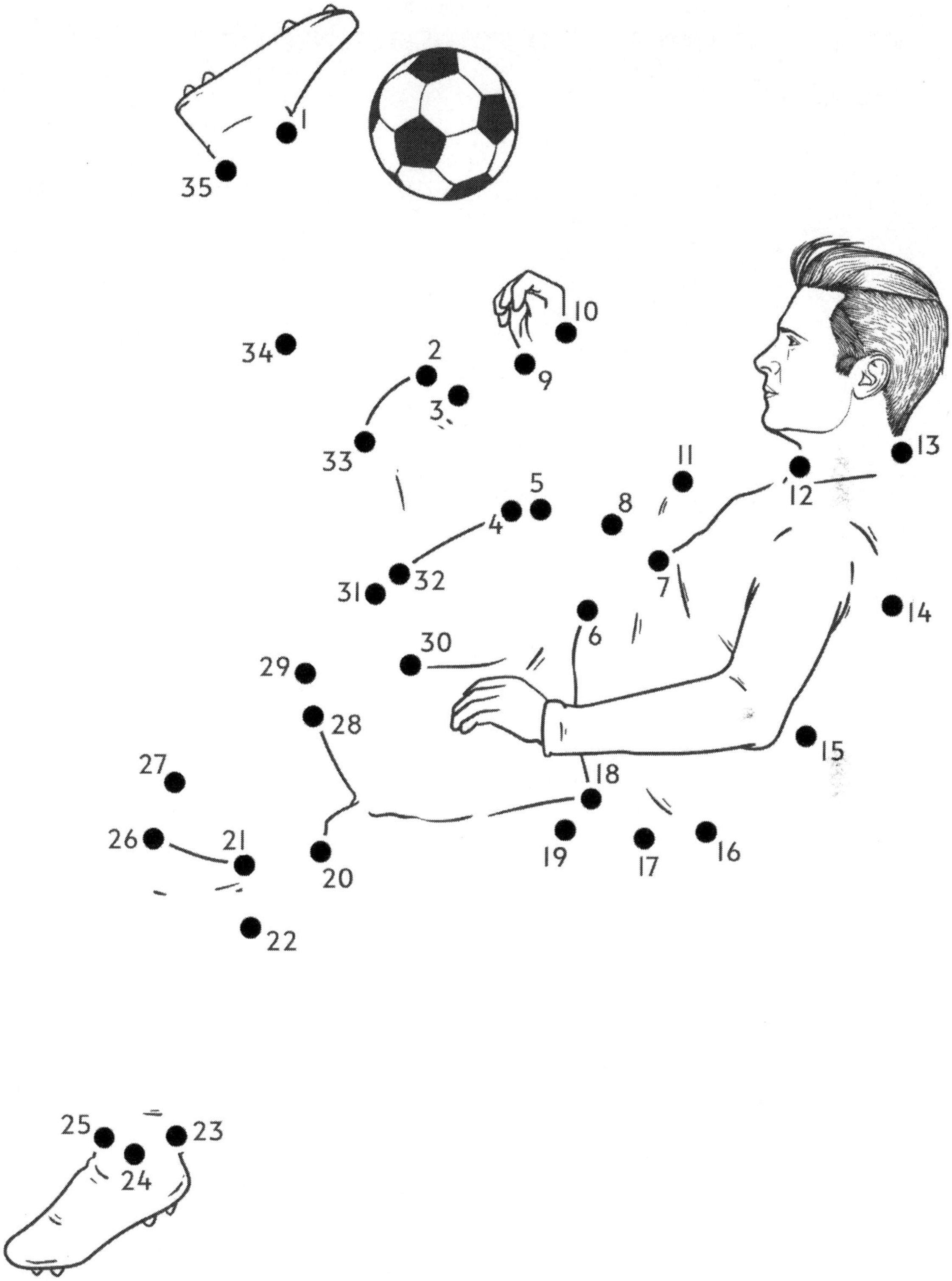
1 2 3 4 5 6 7 8 9 10 11 12 13 14 15 16 17 18 19 20 21 22 23 24 25 26 27 28 29 30 31 32 33 34 35

The club mascot is very happy to see you score that goal. Can you spot the odd one out?

The manager is explaining the tactics for the next match. Unfortunately, all the positions on the board have been scrambled. Unscramble the FIVE positions.

1 ____________________ 2 ____________________

3 ____________________ 4 ____________________

5 ____________________

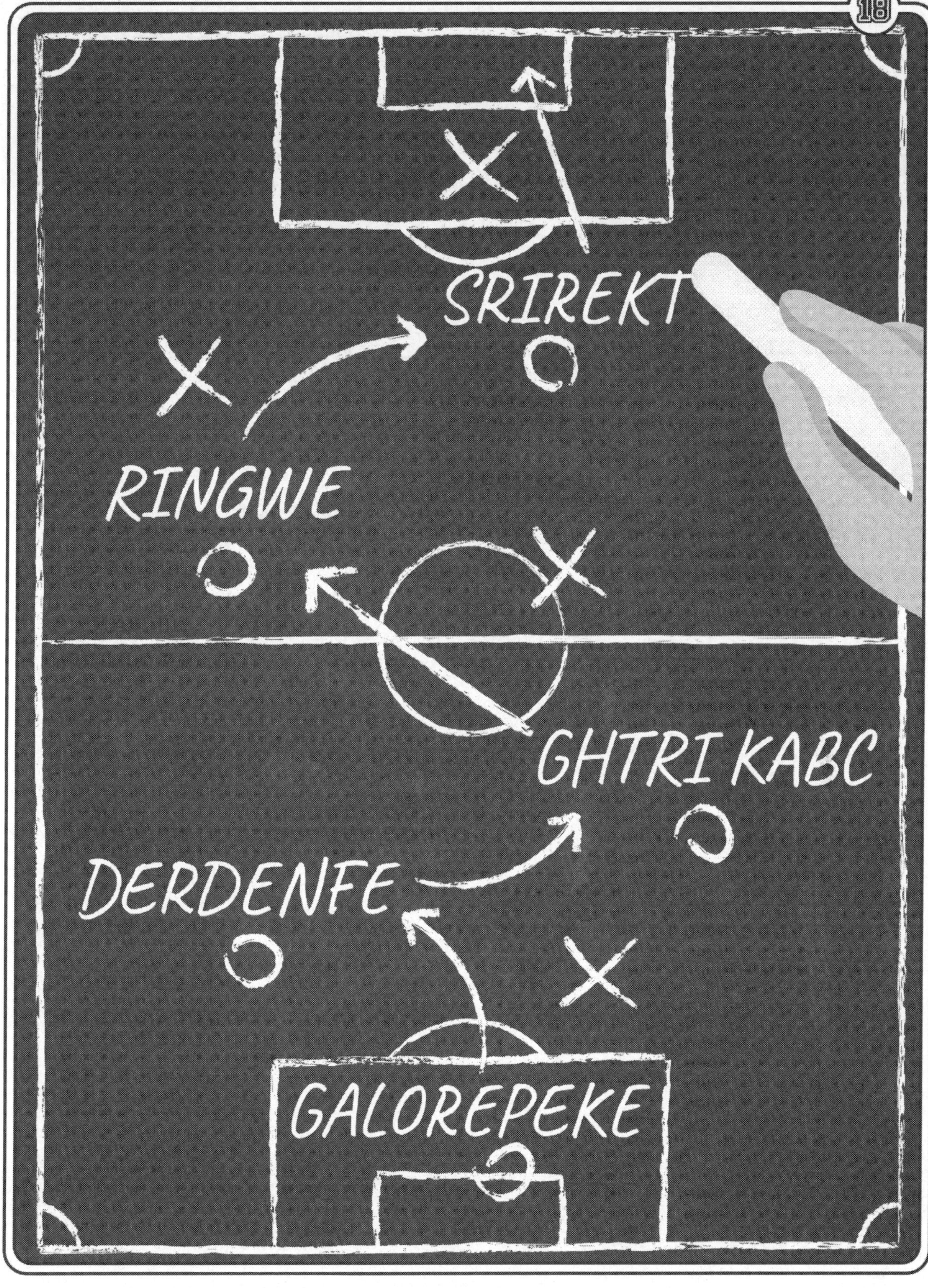
SRIREKT
RINGWE
GHTRI KABC
DERDENFE
GALOREPEKE

After an impressive first half of the season, top division side AFC Warriors have signed you in the winter transfer window. Colour in the page with the colours of your new team.

The manager is explaining the tactics for the next match. Unfortunately, all the positions on the board have been scrambled. Unscramble the FIVE positions.

1 goalkeeper

2 defender

3 right back

4 winger

5 striker

Design a badge for your new team.

DESIGN THE BADGE

Design the shirt for your new team.

Can you spot the SIX differences between the two pictures? When you have spotted all of the differences, colour the tracksuit in your new team's colours.

The manager has asked you to practice your shooting with the goalkeeper. Can you copy the drawing of the goalkeeper's glove? You can then design and colour the gloves.

COMPLETE THE DRAWING

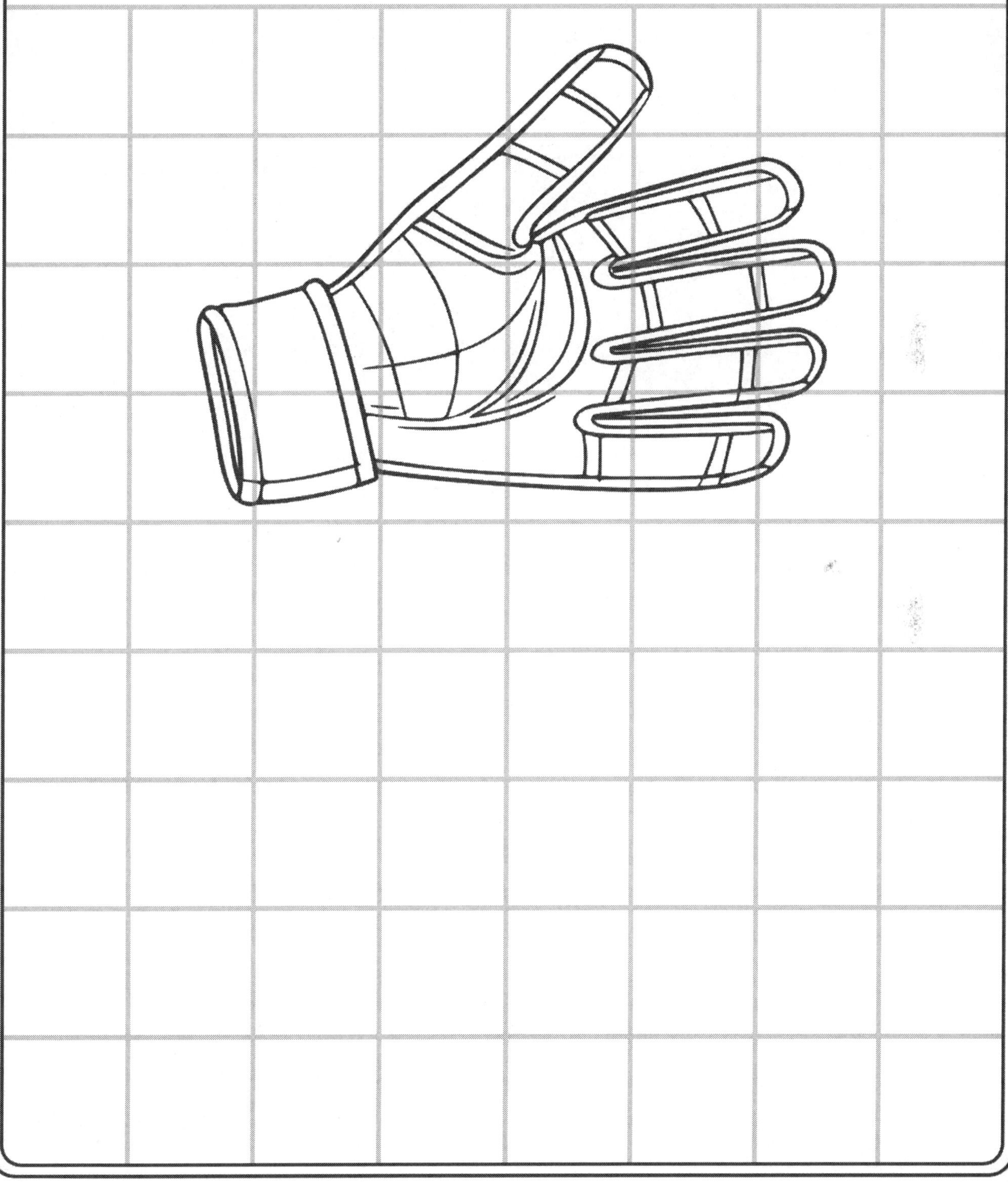

It's the morning of your first match with your new club. After a healthy breakfast, it's time to pack your bag for the big match. Find all the pieces of equipment in the wordsearch.

EQUIPMENT

E	S	P	B	O	O	T	S	T	S	G	O
G	W	S	R	S	O	E	R	E	D	J	C
S	R	O	X	A	H	C	V	B	W	R	W
H	F	C	K	L	R	O	V	X	K	S	H
I	S	K	B	X	L	M	R	H	G	V	I
R	Z	S	K	G	B	N	B	T	L	J	S
T	E	B	O	T	T	L	E	A	S	A	T
N	Y	D	C	I	O	K	K	Q	N	L	L
S	H	I	N	P	A	D	S	C	S	D	E
S	I	G	F	E	Q	Q	F	F	O	Q	N
R	D	M	B	A	L	L	A	U	V	V	X
W	I	L	Y	I	L	T	P	G	B	C	C

BOOTS
SOCKS
SHORTS
SHIRT
SHINPADS
BALL
BOTTLE
GLOVES
ARMBAND
WHISTLE

After a good run in the cup, you've made it all the way to the final. List all the players that have made the starting eleven.

EQUIPMENT

E	S	P	B	O	O	T	S	T	S	G	O
G	W	S	R	S	O	E	R	E	D	J	C
S	R	O	X	A	H	C	V	B	W	R	W
H	F	C	K	L	R	O	V	X	K	S	H
I	S	K	B	X	L	M	R	H	G	V	I
R	Z	S	K	G	B	N	B	T	L	J	S
T	E	B	O	T	T	L	E	A	S	A	T
N	Y	D	C	I	O	K	K	Q	N	L	L
S	H	I	N	P	A	D	S	C	S	D	E
S	I	G	F	E	Q	Q	F	F	O	Q	N
R	D	M	B	A	L	L	A	U	V	V	X
W	I	L	Y	I	L	T	P	G	B	C	C

BOOTS
SOCKS
SHORTS
SHIRT
SHINPADS
BALL
BOTTLE
GLOVES
ARMBAND
WHISTLE

STARTING LINEUP

After a tense first half, the score is 0-0. Collect the ball, make your way through the maze, past the defenders and score the winning goal.

A national sport website has written an article about your match winning performance in the cup final. Can you identify the missing letters?

___ ___ ___ ___ ___ ___

AMB SPORT

FOOTBALL > CUP FINAL

In a showdown that had everyone on the edge of their seats, the _eam with fantastic teamwork and skills emerged victorious, proudly lifting the trophy. The crowd erupted in cheers as they watched this _emarkable team showcase their talents.

The most breathtaking moment came in the 53rd minute _f the game when the star player performed some magic on the field. He dribbled _ast not one, not two, but three defenders to score the winning goal. It was a jaw-dropping move that left everyone very _appy.

This victory isn't just about a trophy; it's about the power of teamwork, determination, and believing in _ourself.

RED CARD! In your next league match, a late tackle on an opposing player has forced the referee to send you off. Connect the dots to draw the referee and then colour him in... and the red card.

Your debut performance has made the front page of the local newspaper. Due to an error, some letters are missing from the article. Can you identify the missing letters to create a word?

t r o p h y

1
2
3
4
5
6
7
8
9
10
11
12
13
14
15
16
17
18
19
20
21

You have been suspended for one match after being sent off. You have to watch the next match from a seat in the stands. Can you complete the drawing and colour it in?

The team struggled without you and went on to lose the match. The manager has prepared a tough training session to try and improve the team. The SIX parts of the training session have not been spelled correctly. Can you rearrange the letters to work out the SIX parts of the training session? Each one has a clue to help you.

TRAINING SESSION

1. MRWA PU > ________________
Gentle exercises to make our bodies ready to run and play safely.

2. DRGIBBILN > ________________
Using our feet to move the soccer ball around the field while we control it.

3. GINPASS > ________________
Sharing the ball with our teammates by kicking it to them so we can work together.

4. GOOTHINS > ________________
Kicking the football firmly and accurately into the goal.

5. CLINGKAT > ________________
We use our feet and skills to try and take the soccer ball away from an opponent on the other team.

6. CMHAT > ________________
We use everything we've learned in our soccer training to play a game with our teammates.

You're lining up to take a free kick. Can you spot the FIVE differences between the two images?

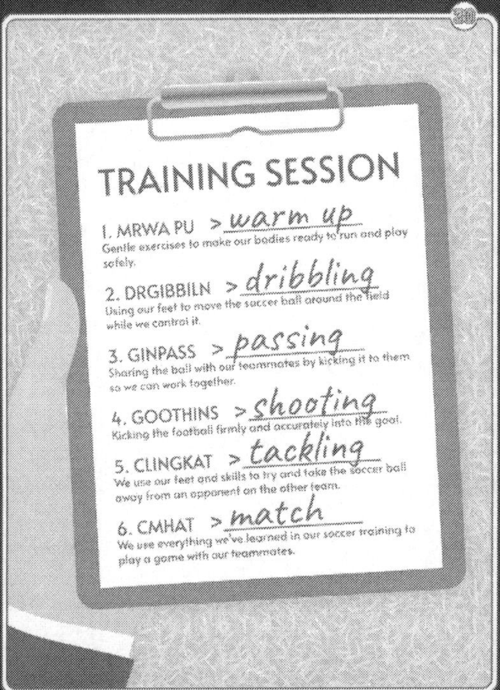

Congratulations! Your impressive peformances have resulted in the national team manager selecting you for your country. This is every young footballer's dream. There are lots of words to describe how you feel, can you find them all in the wordsearch?

INTERNATIONAL DEBUT

H	D	E	T	E	R	M	I	N	E	D	U
R	M	G	P	R	I	D	E	G	L	D	N
O	I	H	O	A	T	H	U	M	B	L	E
C	X	P	Q	O	T	H	A	P	P	Y	B
N	I	U	G	E	S	P	M	N	I	D	R
C	K	S	B	X	R	E	S	P	E	C	T
Y	J	B	N	C	W	J	B	A	J	Z	S
X	X	O	S	I	D	R	W	U	B	W	Z
T	D	F	Y	T	T	Q	E	M	M	D	A
Y	K	G	N	E	R	V	O	U	S	P	C
E	U	Y	E	D	I	Y	W	A	X	J	S
G	R	A	T	I	T	U	D	E	D	P	B

EXCITED
PRIDE
JOY
NERVOUS
GRATITUDE
DETERMINED
GOOSEBUMPS
RESPECT
HUMBLE
HAPPY

Design your country's kit. After coming on as a substitute, you helped your country to a 2-2 draw in their final match before the summer's international cup.

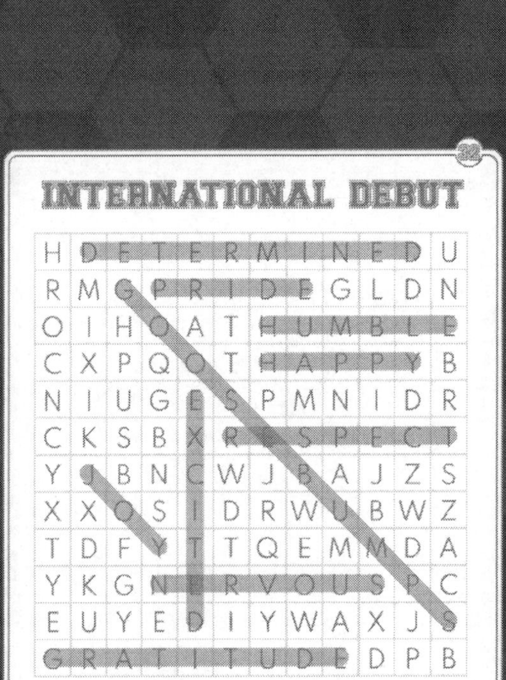
INTERNATIONAL DEBUT

H	D	E	T	E	R	M	I	N	E	D	U
R	M	G	P	R	I	D	E	G	L	D	N
O	I	H	O	A	T	H	U	M	B	L	E
C	X	P	Q	O	T	H	A	P	P	Y	B
N	I	U	G	E	S	P	M	N	I	D	R
C	K	S	B	X	R	E	S	P	E	C	T
Y	J	B	N	C	W	J	B	A	J	Z	S
X	X	O	S	I	D	R	W	U	B	W	Z
T	D	F	Y	T	T	Q	E	M	M	D	A
Y	K	G	N	E	R	V	O	U	S	P	C
E	U	Y	E	D	I	Y	W	A	X	J	S
G	R	A	T	I	T	U	D	E	D	P	B

EXCITED
PRIDE
JOY
NERVOUS
GRATITUDE
DETERMINED
GOOSEBUMPS
RESPECT
HUMBLE
HAPPY

It's the final match of the season for your club. You need to avoid defeat to win the league title. After 90 minutes, it's 0-0. An opposing player is about to score a goal, get the boot through the maze and tackle him before you lose the match!

CHAMPIONS! After making the tackle and drawing 0-0, you have won the league trophy. Can you spot the odd one out?

That's the end of the league season. As we look ahead to the international cup in the summer, can you match the words to create the footballing phrases?

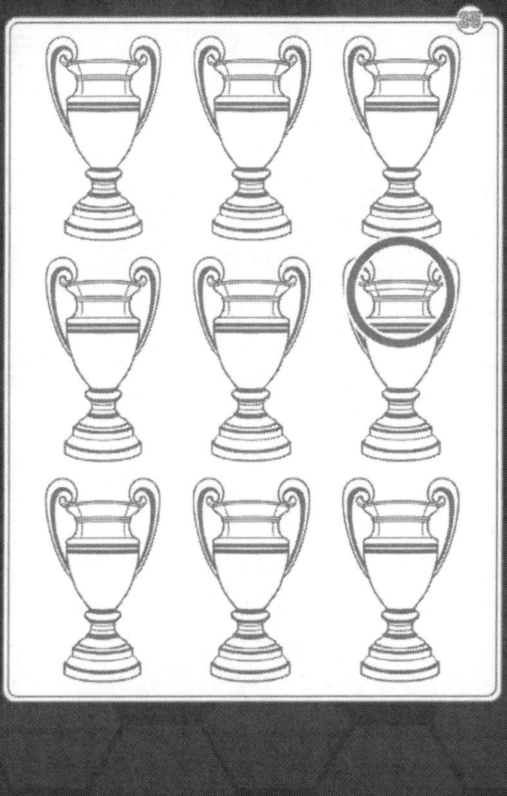

MATCH THE WORDS

Golden

Yellow

Corner

Goalie

Throw

Time

Extra

Penalty

Wasting

Time

Spot

Boot

Card

In

Gloves

Flag

Design the official ball of the international cup.

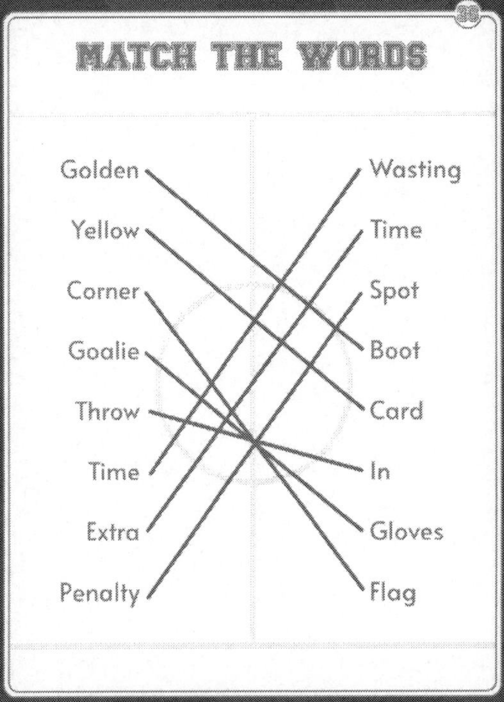

DESIGN THE FOOTBALL

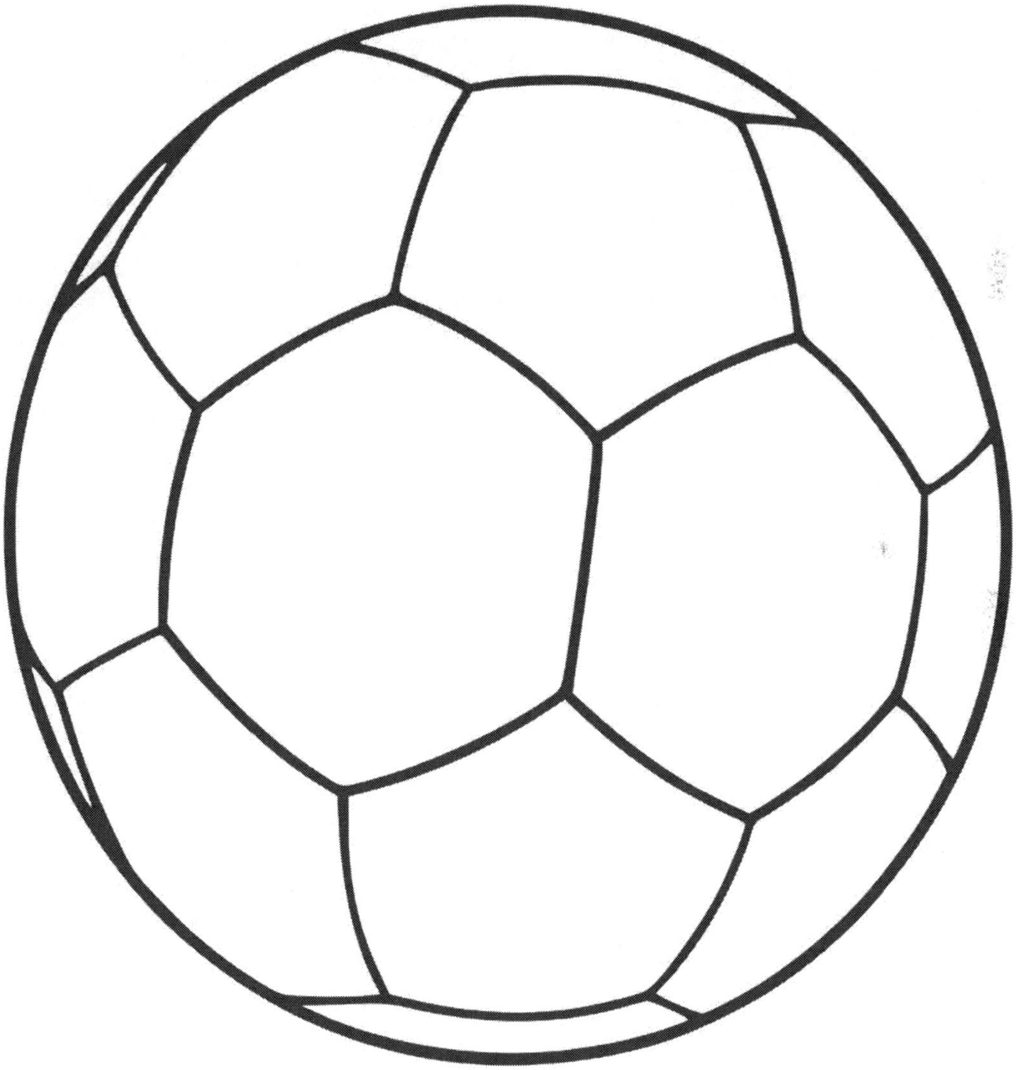

There are 16 countries playing in the international cup. Can you find 15 of them in the word search? There is also a space to add the final country of your choice to Group D.

INTERNATIONAL CUP

Q	F	H	O	K	L	M	E	X	I	C	O
Z	M	O	R	O	C	C	O	P	A	E	V
H	N	X	R	R	U	Z	X	O	X	L	I
S	I	F	R	A	N	C	E	R	E	L	V
P	G	L	A	R	G	E	N	T	I	N	A
A	E	E	W	W	C	N	X	U	M	I	B
I	R	V	R	I	A	G	B	G	Q	R	R
N	I	W	Y	M	X	L	R	A	H	E	A
X	A	V	S	Q	A	A	E	L	N	L	Z
I	T	A	L	Y	A	N	S	S	B	A	I
J	A	P	A	N	K	D	Y	L	D	N	L
Z	P	S	C	O	T	L	A	N	D	D	Z

GROUP A

ENGLAND
ARGENTINA
FRANCE
NIGERIA

GROUP B

BRAZIL
ITALY
SCOTLAND
JAPAN

GROUP C

PORTUGAL
MEXICO
SPAIN
IRELAND

GROUP D

WALES
GERMANY
MOROCCO
____

Can you unscramble the letters to work out each country from the first round of group matches?

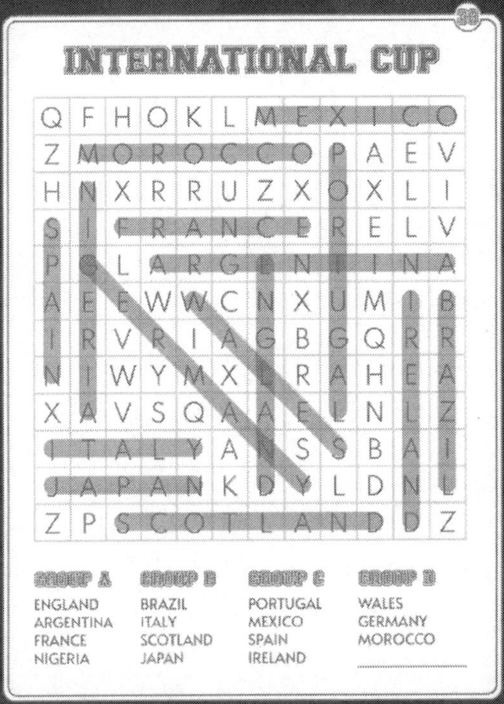

38

INTERNATIONAL CUP

Q	F	H	O	K	L	M	E	X	I	C	O
Z	M	O	R	O	C	C	O	P	A	E	V
H	N	X	R	R	U	Z	X	O	X	L	I
S	I	F	R	A	N	C	E	R	E	L	V
P	G	L	A	R	G	E	N	T	I	N	A
A	E	E	W	W	C	N	X	U	M	I	B
I	R	V	R	I	A	G	B	G	Q	R	R
N	I	W	Y	M	X	L	R	A	H	E	A
X	A	V	S	Q	A	A	E	L	N	L	Z
I	T	A	L	Y	A	N	S	S	B	A	I
J	A	P	A	N	K	D	Y	L	D	N	L
Z	P	S	C	O	T	L	A	N	D	D	Z

GROUP A	GROUP B	GROUP C	GROUP D
ENGLAND	BRAZIL	PORTUGAL	WALES
ARGENTINA	ITALY	MEXICO	GERMANY
FRANCE	SCOTLAND	SPAIN	MOROCCO
NIGERIA	JAPAN	IRELAND	

MATCH RESULTS

GROUP A

ERFANC 0 v 2 DENLANG

____________ ____________

GROUP B

ANTCOLDS 2 v 1 ANAPJ

____________ ____________

GROUP C

CMIEOX 2 v 3 DERNAIL

____________ ____________

GROUP D

AWLSE 1 v 0 MEGANYR

____________ ____________

You've made it past the group stage and in to the quarter-final. Your home kit is similar to the home kit of the other country so you'll need to play in the away kit. Design the away kit for your country.

MATCH RESULTS

GROUP A

ERFANC 0 v 2 DENLANG

France England

GROUP B

ANTCOLDS 2 v 1 ANAPJ

Scotland Japan

GROUP C

CMIEOX 2 v 3 DERNAIL

Mexico Ireland

GROUP D

AWLSE 1 v 0 MEGANYR

Wales Germany

After winning the quarter-final, you're in the semi-final. There is a feature about you in the matchday programme. Can you find the missing letters?

__ __ __ __ __ __ __

PLAYER
profile

Every day after school, he'd rush to the _ark with his football. He practiced kicking, running, and g_tting better with each try. Even when it was raining, he'd find a spot indoors to practice. He never gave up, liste_ed to his coaches, and always tried his best. As he grew older, his skills improved, and one d_y, his dream came true, he became a professiona_ football player, jus_ like in his wildest dreams. Remember, with hard work and believing in _ourself, anything is possible!

You've made it all the way to the final and the stadium is ready. Spot the SEVEN differences between the two pictures.

After winning the quarter final, you're in the semi final. There is a feature about you in the matchday programme. Can you find the missing letters?

p e n a l t y

Select the starting lineup for the final.

STARTING LINEUP

The manager has made you captain for the final. Make your way through the maze to collect the captain's armband.

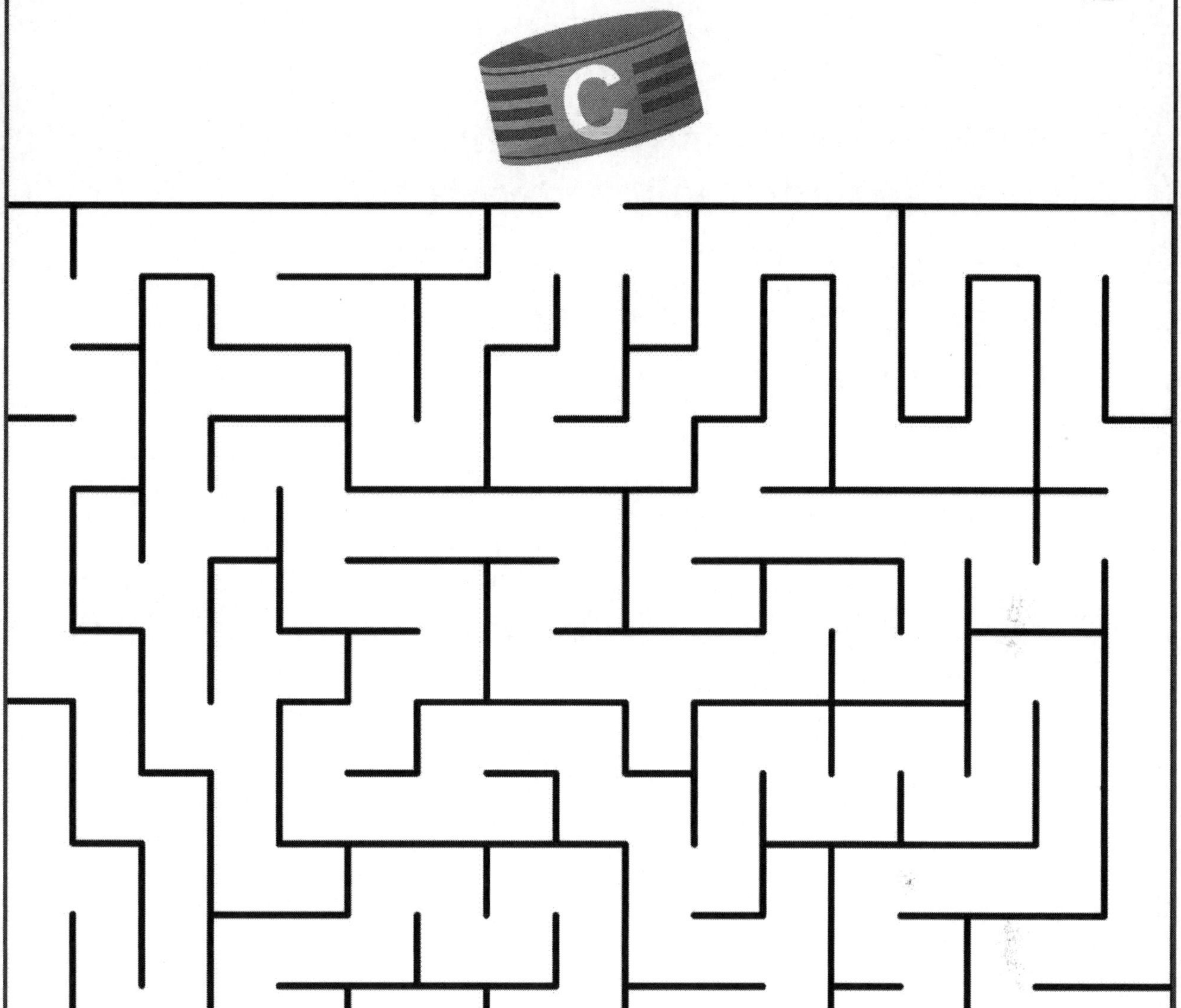
C

It all comes down to this. After 90 minutes of normal time, and 30 minutes of extra time, the match will be decided by penalties. Connect the dots and step up to take your penalty. Once complete, colour the picture in.

21
1
2
3
20
4
5
17
19
18
16
6
15
7
8
11
13
9
14
10
12

CHAMPIONS OF THE WORLD!

Complete the drawing and lift the trophy.

COMPLETE THE DRAWING

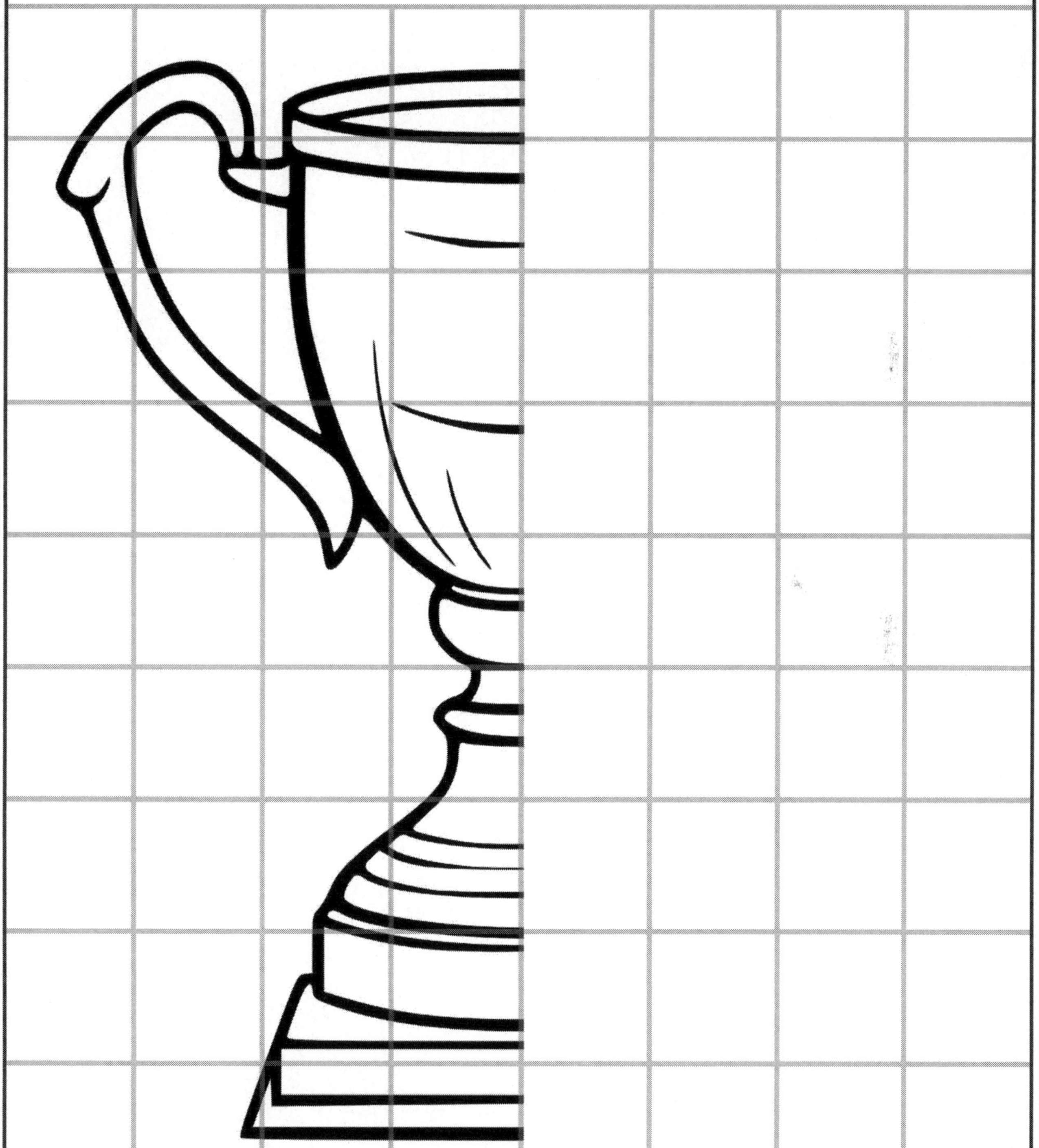

After scoring the winning penalty, you've won the trophy for your country. Which image is the odd one out?

These fans are so happy to meet their hero. Sign an autograph for them.

CAREER STATISTICS

Complete your career statistics below

Club appearances: ....

Club goals: ....

Club assists: ....

League titles: ....

Domestic trophies: ....

Continental trophies: ....

Total transfer fees: £ ....

Player of the match awards: ....

International appearances: ....

International goals: ....

International assists: ....

International trophies: ....

Best player in the world awards: ....

Time for the final challenge. There's only one word to find, how quickly can you find it?

FINAL CHALLENGE

C	H	N	I	I	I	H	P	I	C	A	M
A	C	O	O	C	M	H	O	C	C	A	A
O	N	P	I	P	A	H	A	O	H	N	M
C	C	P	P	C	I	I	M	M	I	P	H
O	M	C	M	M	H	N	A	M	I	C	O
M	I	P	H	P	N	N	A	N	N	O	H
I	M	A	I	A	I	N	O	I	P	H	I
O	N	I	P	H	M	H	P	O	A	A	P
H	M	P	N	H	A	P	C	I	P	I	C
O	N	C	A	I	I	C	I	I	I	P	A
N	A	M	I	O	C	P	H	O	I	P	H
O	O	M	P	O	H	A	N	O	N	M	O

CHAMPION

FINAL CHALLENGE

C	H	N	I	I	I	H	P	I	C	A	M
A	C	O	O	C	M	H	O	C	C	A	A
O	N	P	I	P	A	H	A	O	H	N	M
C	C	P	P	C	I	I	M	M	I	P	H
O	M	C	M	M	H	N	A	M	I	C	O
M	I	P	H	P	N	N	A	N	N	O	H
I	M	A	I	A	I	N	O	I	P	H	I
O	N	I	P	H	M	H	P	O	A	A	P
H	M	P	N	H	A	P	C	I	P	I	C
O	N	C	A	I	I	C	I	I	I	P	A
N	A	M	I	O	C	P	H	O	I	P	H
O	O	M	P	O	H	A	N	O	N	M	O

CHAMPION

Printed in Great Britain
by Amazon

39743050R00059